D1416690

TRAINS

TRAVELING MACHINES

Jason Cooper

Rourke Enterprises, Inc.
Vero Beach, Florida 32964

PHOTO CREDITS

© Lynn M. Stone

LIBRARY OF CONGRESS
Library of Congress Cataloging-in-Publication Data
Cooper, Jason, 1942-
   Trains / by Jason Cooper.
   p. cm. — (Traveling machines)
   Includes index.
   Summary: Examines the history, varieties, and uses of trains.
   ISBN 0-86592-490-2
   1. Railroads—Juvenile literature. [1. Railroads.] I. Title.
II. Series: Cooper, Jason, 1942-   Traveling machines.
TF148.C59   1991
625.1—dc20   90-26926
                    CIP
                    AC

Printed in the USA

TABLE OF CONTENTS

TRAINS

A train is a group of railroad cars pulled or pushed by a **locomotive** over steel rails. Trains transport people and products called **freight.**

Train locomotives and cars have wheels with special edges. The shape of the wheels keeps the train on the rails.

Train cars and locomotives are attached to each other by **couplers.** Together the locomotive and cars travel over the path of the rails. Some rails are in tunnels and on bridges.

Early morning commuter train in Old Saybrook, Connecticut

RAILROADS

Train rails are set onto wooden or concrete **ties.** The two rails, always the same distance apart, make up the **track.** The track lies on hard, raised ground known as **roadbed.** The track and roadbed are often called the railroad.

Railroad also refers to any company that operates trains. The United States has about 500 railroad companies and 170,000 miles of track. In most countries, the railroads are owned by the country.

The longest American railroad is the Burlington Northern.

Burlington Northern freight train passing through snow shed in Rocky Mountains

EARLY TRAINS AND RAILROADS

The first American trains with locomotives began service in 1830. These early trains were pulled and pushed by steam-powered engines.

One of the first engines, the *Tom Thumb*, was defeated by a horse in a race. But locomotives improved, and train service in the East grew quickly. By 1869, a railroad passenger could travel 3,000 miles from the east coast to the west coast of the United States.

Old steam engines on view at the Illinois Railway Museum, Union, Illinois

MODERN TRAINS AND RAILROADS

Trains became longer and faster over the years. Wooden cars were replaced by steel cars. But after World War II ended in 1945, people traveled more and more often by car and airplane. Many railroads were forced to give up passenger service. They were losing too much money. A new company, Amtrak, took over most passenger service throughout the country.

Passenger traffic is starting to grow again, but American trains continue to haul mostly freight.

Amtrak California Zephyr
westbound from Chicago

Chicago and Northwestern Railroad freight train

Burlington Northern Railroad freight yard and Chicago skyline

STEAM LOCOMOTIVES

Steam locomotives have big, powerful driving wheels and tall smoke stacks. Until the late 1800s, all American train engines were steam locomotives. A few railroads then turned to electric engines.

Steam engines are followed by a **tender.** The tender carries the locomotive's fuel—wood, oil, or coal. The burning fuel puffs clouds of smoke from the smoke stack.

By 1960, American steam locomotives had nearly disappeared.

*St. Louis-San Francisco
Railroad steam engine*

DIESEL LOCOMOTIVES

Diesel locomotives began to replace steam in the 1930s. Nearly all American locomotives in service today—some 27,000 of them—are diesels.

Diesel locomotives burn oil. They are faster, more powerful, and less costly than steam engines. They can travel long distances without having to stop for fuel or service.

Like steam locomotives, diesels are operated by an **engineer** who rides in the locomotive cab.

*Burlington Route diesel
engine of the 1940s*

PASSENGER TRAINS

Commuter trains carry passengers short distances. Long-distance Amtrak passenger trains have many kinds of cars: sleepers, dining cars, lounge cars, and glass-topped dome cars.

Amtrak trains use many of the routes and names of famous trains from the past, like the *California Zephyr*, which travels from Chicago to California.

The *Zephyr* and other American trains rarely travel faster than 80 miles per hour. The Japanese have a speedy "bullet" train, however, and the French have an even faster train that reaches 190 miles per hour.

Doubledeck commuter cars at station in Aurora, Illinois

FREIGHT TRAINS

American railroads earn most of their money by hauling freight. On an average day, 10,000 freight cars rumble across the United States.

Freight cars carry coal, grain, lumber, automobiles, truck trailers, fruit, and many other things. The **caboose** cars, which used to be at the end of freight trains, are rarely used now.

Long freights may be over two miles long with over 200 cars pulled by 8 locomotives.

Burlington Northern freight train on trestle near Essex, Montana

THE WONDER OF TRAINS

The sights and sounds of trains delight people. When a train leaves a station, it hisses and growls and shakes the earth. Like a galloping iron horse, it roars toward a railroad crossing. The locomotive's yellow light grows larger. Its horn blasts. Bells ring and red lights wink on the gates.

The cars race by—clickety-clack, clickety-clack. Suddenly the train has passed, rolling its thunder down the tracks.

Glossary

caboose (kah BOOSE) — a car used by part of a train's crew and attached to the end of a freight train

commuter (kah MEW ter) — a passenger train operating between a large city and its suburbs

coupler (KUP ler) — a device that links with another like it and attaches two train cars

engineer (en gin EAR) — the person who rides in the cab of a train locomotive and operates the train

freight (FRAYT) — the goods hauled by a train or the train that hauls such goods, or cargo

locomotive (lo ko MO tiv) — a self-powered vehicle that runs on rails and hauls railroad cars

roadbed (RODE bed) — the hard, raised surface on which railroad ties and rails (track) rest

tender (TEN der) — a railroad car that carries fuel for the locomotive

tie (TIE) — a concrete or wooden support to which railroad rails are fastened so that they remain in line

track (TRAK) — the two rails on which a train rides and their pathway

INDEX